RAIN FOREST

RAIN FOREST

PHOTOGRAPHED BY
FRANK GREENAWAY

WRITTEN BY
BARBARA TAYLOR

DK PUBLISHING, INC.

DK

A DK PUBLISHING BOOK
www.dk.com

Project editor Christiane Gunzi **Art editor** Val Wright
Editorial assistant Deborah Murrell **Designer** Julie Staniland
Design assistant Nicola Rawson
Production Louise Barratt
Illustrations Nick Hall, Nick Hewetson, Dan Wright
Additional editorial assistance Jill Somerscales
Managing editor Sophie Mitchell
Managing art editor Miranda Kennedy

Consultants
Barry Clarke, Andy Currant, Theresa Greenaway, Paul Hillyard,
Judith Marshall, Tim Parmenter, Edward Wade, Kathie Way

Endpapers photographed by M.P.L. Fogden, Bruce Coleman Ltd.

First American Edition, 1992
First Paperback Edition, 1998

4 6 8 10 7 5 3

Published in the United States by
DK Publishing, Inc., 95 Madison Avenue, New York, New York 10016.

Library of Congress Cataloging-in-Publication Data
Taylor, Barbara, 1954-
Rain forest/by Barbara Taylor. – 1st American ed.
p. cm. – (Look closer)
Includes index.
Summary: Examines the variety of life found in a rain forest, including the flying gecko,
poison dart frog, and curly-haired tarantula.
ISBN 0-7894-2971-3
1. Rain forest fauna – Juvenile literature. 2. Rain forest plants – Juvenile literature. (1. Rain forest animals.).
I. Title. II. Series: Taylor, Barbara, 1954-
Look closer.
QL 112.T39 1992
591.909'52–dc20

Color reproduction by Colourscan, Singapore
Printed and bound in Singapore by Imago

CONTENTS

Look for us, and we will show you the size of every animal and plant that you read about in this book.

LIFE IN A RAIN FOREST

AN ASTONISHING VARIETY of wildlife leaps, flies, or crawls in the damp, shady world of the rain forest. Most of the animals live high up in the trees, where there is more sunlight and rain. Leaves, twigs, rotten wood, and animal droppings fall to the forest floor, where thousands of smaller creatures scuttle or slither around. Many rain forests have been cut down for lumber or to clear the land for farms and factories. We need to protect the forests that are left for the sake of the animals and plants that live there.

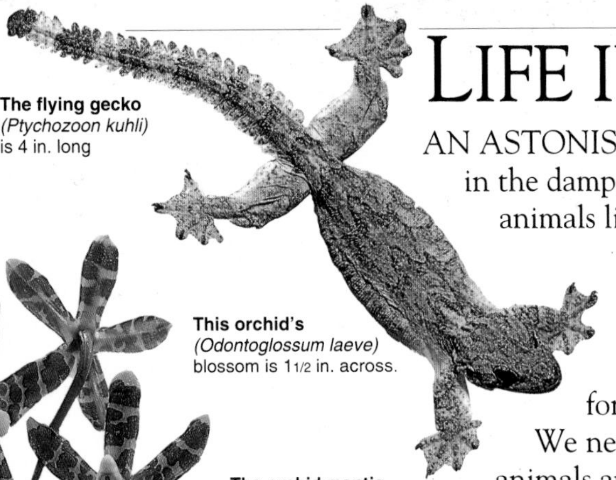

The flying gecko
(Ptychozoon kuhli)
is 4 in. long

This orchid's
(Odontoglossum laeve)
blossom is 1 1/2 in. across.

The orchid mantis
(Hymenopus coronatus)
is 2 1/2 in. long.

The postman butterfly
(Heliconius melpomene)
is 1 1/4 in. across its wings.

The passion flower's
(Passiflora caerulea)
blossom is 3 in. across.

This orchid's
(Encyclia pentotis)
blossom is 2 1/4 in. across.

The postman caterpillar
(Heliconius melpomene)
is 1 in. long

The tiger centipede
(Scolopendra gigantea) is
9 1/2 in. long.

The Cuvier's toucan's (*Ramphastos cuvieri*) beak is 5 in. long.

The Franquet's fruit bat (*Epomops franqueti*) has a wingspan of 14 in.

The White's tree frog (*Litoria caerulea*) is 2 1/2 in. long.

The curly-haired tarantula (*Brachypelma albopilosa*) is 3 1/2 in. across.

The poison dart frog (*Dendrobates truncatus*) is 1 in. long

GLIDING GECKO

THE FLYING GECKO lives high up in the rain forest trees. This lizard does not really fly, but its body has adapted so that it can glide from tree to tree to escape danger. Flying geckos are active mainly at night, when it is cooler. Their excellent eyesight and hearing help them to find insects to eat. Geckos lay one or two eggs with soft, sticky shells. They often hide the eggs under tree bark until the shells harden. The young geckos take several months to develop within their eggs. Eventually, they break their way out by using the pointed egg tooth on their snout.

The eyes have a fixed, transparent covering. Most other lizards have movable eyelids.

These mottled colors disguise the gecko against the bark and leaves in the forest.

A gecko clicks its tongue against the roof of its mouth when courting a mate or defending territory.

These flaps of skin act as parachutes when the gecko leaps from tree to tree.

If the tail is broken off, a new one slowly grows to replace it.

NIGHT SIGHT
The pupils of the eyes open wide to help the gecko to see in the dark. In daylight, they close to a slit to protect the sensitive eyes from the light. The gecko cannot blink to clean its eyes but wipes them clean with its tongue.

LEATHER PARACHUTE
Flaps of leathery skin along the sides of the gecko's body and tail can spread out like wings for gliding. This makes the lizard's body flatter and wider, so it falls more slowly through the air. A parachute slows down a person's fall from an airplane in a similar way.

The gecko spreads its feet out as wide as possible for gliding.

Webbing between the toes helps the gecko steer as it glides.

Sharp claws and long toes cling to the bark of trees.

SCALY TOES
Each of the gecko's toes has a flat pad covered with ridges of scales. On these scales are many thousands of microscopic hairs that point backward. When the gecko presses its feet against a surface, the hairs stick in the cracks and pits, giving the lizard a glue-like grip.

Ridges of scales under the feet enable the gecko to cling to slippery surfaces, even vertical ones.

GUESS WHAT?
A gecko's grip is so strong that it can run upside down along branches. It can cling to a pane of glass so tightly that it cannot be pulled off without breaking the glass.

MURDER BY POISON

LARGE, POISONOUS CENTIPEDES scurry across the floor of the rain forest searching for prey. They feed mainly on insects and spiders, but also catch small toads, snakes, and mammals. Their poison fangs are formidable weapons. Giant tiger centipedes like this one can easily dry out, so they emerge only at night when the forest is cool and damp. During the day, the tiger centipede hides under leaves, logs, and bark where the air is moist. The female digs a hole in the earth under a stone and lays her eggs there. She curls her long body around the eggs to protect them. When they hatch, the young centipedes have just as many legs as their parents. They have to molt (shed their skin) in order to grow, because their hard outer skin, called the exoskeleton, will not stretch as they grow bigger.

Two long, jointed antennae help the centipede to feel its way around and detect food.

These mouthparts tear up food.

On the end of the poison fang, there is a curved tip that injects poison into a victim.

FEARSOME FANGS
Centipedes stun their prey with the large poison claws just below the head. They hold the victim firmly in their fangs and tear it to pieces with their mouthparts. The centipede eats only the soft parts of its prey.

Close up, you can see tiny creatures called mites that live on the centipede.

There are four simple eyes on each side of the head.

Each poison fang has four sections.

LOADS OF LEGS

With its many long legs and flattened body, the centipede can run quickly and smoothly over, under, and around the plants of the rain forest. The legs lift the body off the ground so that it does not catch against leaves or twigs. Tiger centipedes can have as many as 23 pairs of legs.

GUESS WHAT?

Giant tiger centipedes can give humans a very painful bite, much like a hornet sting. But they are not normally dangerous to healthy people.

TOXIC TIGER

Vivid orange and black tiger stripes warn enemies that this centipede is poisonous. Predators soon learn to leave it alone.

Claws on the ends of the legs grip onto trees and rocks.

Two large legs at the end of the abdomen hold the centipede's prey still while it injects poison into it.

The legs are attached to the sides of the body.

These jointed legs bend easily.

A hard exoskeleton protects the soft inner body.

The bright colors warn other animals that the centipede is poisonous.

Each segment of the body has one breathing hole, called a spiracle.

GLUED TO THE SPOT

THE DAMP, SHADY RAIN FOREST makes an ideal home for frogs. They need to live in moist places because their skin is not waterproof and it dries out quickly. Frogs also need pools of water for their tadpoles to live in while they grow into adults. In the rain forest, some frogs lay their eggs on a leaf or a patch of ground that they have carefully cleared. When the tadpoles of poison dart frogs hatch out, they wriggle on to one of their parent's backs. The adult frog carries the tadpoles to a pool of water in the center of the leaves of plants called bromeliads. Tree frogs and poison dart frogs have large, sticky suckers on their fingers and toes. The suckers help them to cling onto smooth, wet leaves and mossy branches. In fact, tree frogs can cling upside down in the forest for hours on end.

Two large eyes allow the frog to see well in daylight and also at night when it hunts for food.

The wide mouth houses a sticky tongue for catching beetles, moths, and other insects.

The skin on the frog's throat expands like a balloon to make a loud mating call.

FLABBY FROG

White's tree frogs are often very fat, with folds of flesh on their bodies. The skin on their bellies is loose and helps the frogs to grip as they climb up slippery tree trunks. Many tree frogs are green or brown to help them blend in with the colors of the forest and hide from enemies. Tree frogs usually hide by day and come out only at night.

These long, thin toes curl around leaves and twigs for a strong hold.

Whenever the frog blinks, its eyelids move across the eyes to wipe them clean.

There is an eardrum on each side of the head. The frog can hear a wide range of sounds.

GUESS WHAT?
South American Indians use the poison from poison dart frogs to tip their hunting darts. White's tree frogs have such big appetites that they sometimes eat rats.

DON'T EAT ME
The poison dart frog's brilliant colors warn enemies that it is dangerous. These frogs have special glands in their skin that produce a deadly poison. The poison can paralyze a bird or monkey immediately, so those animals soon learn to leave the frogs alone. The most deadly kind of dart frog contains enough poison to kill six people.

A poison dart frog's brilliant warning colors may be yellow, red, green, or blue.

STICKY FEET
Each finger and toe has a pad on the underside. These pads produce a sticky substance called mucus. The sticky mucus helps the frog to grip wet leaves and other slimy surfaces. With their sticky feet, tree frogs can even climb up slippery tree trunks.

Sticky pads on each finger

EATING MACHINE

IT IS HARD TO BELIEVE that this pale, spiky postman caterpillar will change into a brightly colored butterfly. A caterpillar is in the feeding and growing stage in the life cycle of a butterfly. It hatches out of an egg, often eating its own eggshell. Then it chews its way through huge amounts of leaves. Every few days the caterpillar molts so that its body can grow larger. After about three weeks, it stops eating and turns into a pupa, or chrysalis. The pupa hangs on a silken thread under a leaf. It cannot eat or drink. Inside the pupa, the caterpillar's body breaks down into a liquid. From the liquid, the body of the butterfly forms, then it emerges from the pupa. This fantastic change, from caterpillar to butterfly, is called metamorphosis.

BREATHING TUBES
Like all insects, the caterpillar breathes through holes called spiracles, which are found along the sides of its body. These holes lead to a network of internal tubes called tracheae. In dry weather, the spiracles can close to stop water from escaping the body.

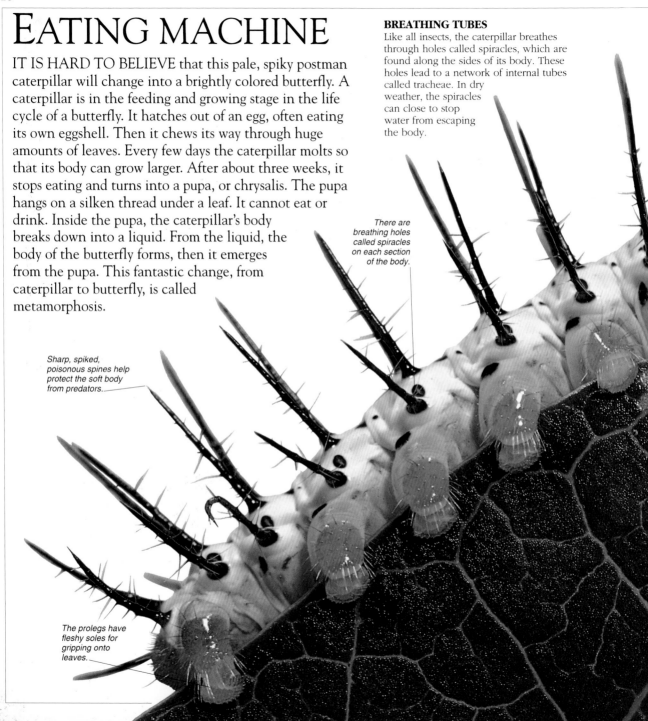

There are breathing holes called spiracles on each section of the body.

Sharp, spiked, poisonous spines help protect the soft body from predators.

The prolegs have fleshy soles for gripping onto leaves.

BAGGY LEGS
The caterpillar's body is like a long, soft bag. To support this bag, there are six true legs on the thorax and ten simple legs called prolegs on the abdomen. The prolegs are covered in hairs, and they have fleshy soles for gripping onto slippery leaves.

GUESS WHAT?
In the three weeks before it pupates, the postman caterpillar eats about 25,000 times its own weight in passionflower leaves.

These six tiny simple eyes on either side of the head can sense whether it is light or dark.

These antennae give the caterpillar a good sense of smell.

PASSIONFLOWER
This passionflower provides food for both the caterpillar and the adult postman butterfly. Adults feed on the nectar and pollen from the flower, and caterpillars eat the leaves. The female butterfly also lays her eggs on the passionflower plant.

There are five bags of yellow pollen that insects brush against when they are feeding on nectar in the base of the flower.

Three stigmas on the ends of stalks collect the pollen carried on the bodies of insects from other flowers.

Strong, muscular jaws for biting and crunching leaves

The caterpillar pulls itself along on its six true legs.

POISONED FOOD
The postman caterpillar feeds on passionflower leaves, which contain poisonous chemicals. The caterpillar digests these poisons, which become part of its body and make it poisonous. When the caterpillar changes into an adult butterfly, the poisons are passed on, so the adults are poisonous, too.

CRUSHED VELVET

WHEN THIS POSTMAN butterfly pulls itself out of its pupa, its wings are soft, damp, and crushed. It takes about an hour for them to stretch and dry out. The main purpose in the life of adult butterflies is to find a mate and lay eggs. The male postman butterfly takes three months to mature before he can mate. The female lays 400 to 500 eggs because so many of the young caterpillars will be eaten by insects and spiders. She lays about 20 eggs at a time on the tender leaves and shoots of passionflower vines. She avoids plants with other eggs or caterpillars on them because caterpillars often one another.

Close up, you can see the scales, which give the wings their color.

GUESS WHAT?
Most butterflies live for only a few days or weeks. But postman butterflies live for up to nine months because they feed on pollen as well as nectar. Pollen is rich in nutrients, especially proteins.

SCALY WINGS
Each wing is covered with thousands of tiny, overlapping scales, which give the wings their color. Butterflies and moths belong to a group of insects called *Lepidoptera*, which means "scaled wing."

When it is not being used, the proboscis is curled up under the head, out of the way.

Six jointed legs are joined to the middle part of the body, called the thorax.

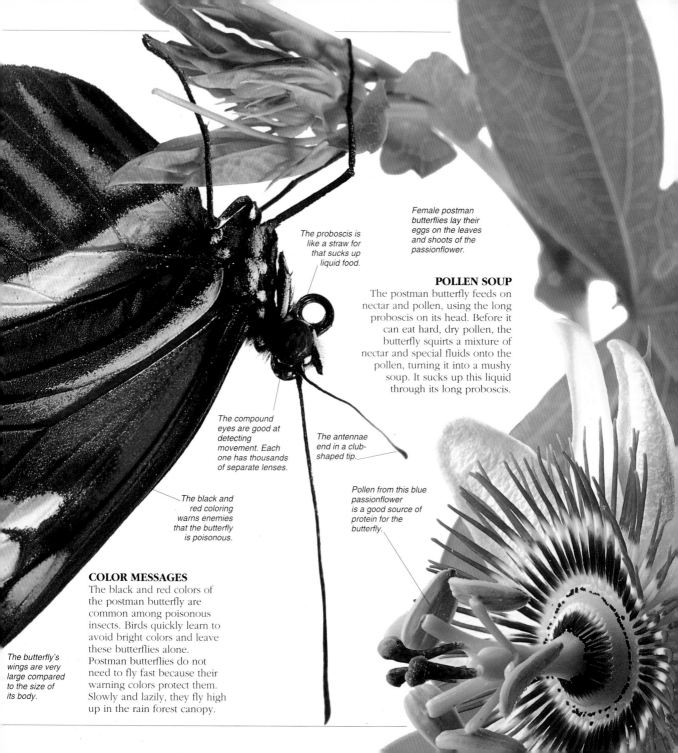

The proboscis is like a straw for that sucks up liquid food.

Female postman butterflies lay their eggs on the leaves and shoots of the passionflower.

POLLEN SOUP
The postman butterfly feeds on nectar and pollen, using the long proboscis on its head. Before it can eat hard, dry pollen, the butterfly squirts a mixture of nectar and special fluids onto the pollen, turning it into a mushy soup. It sucks up this liquid through its long proboscis.

The compound eyes are good at detecting movement. Each one has thousands of separate lenses.

The antennae end in a club-shaped tip.

The black and red coloring warns enemies that the butterfly is poisonous.

Pollen from this blue passionflower is a good source of protein for the butterfly.

COLOR MESSAGES
The black and red colors of the postman butterfly are common among poisonous insects. Birds quickly learn to avoid bright colors and leave these butterflies alone. Postman butterflies do not need to fly fast because their warning colors protect them. Slowly and lazily, they fly high up in the rain forest canopy.

The butterfly's wings are very large compared to the size of its body.

FURRY FLYER

SHY, SECRETIVE fruit bats leave the trees at dusk and fly over the rain forest canopy to search for food. They cannot turn well as they fly, and they prefer to avoid the thick plant growth lower down in the forest. Fruit bats feed mainly on fruits such as figs, mangoes, and bananas. They spit out seeds from these fruits or pass them out in their droppings, and this helps the trees to spread throughout the forest. Many bats live in large groups, but male Franquet's fruit bats usually roost (rest) alone. The females sometimes roost in groups when they are nursing their young. Bats are blind and hairless when they are born. They cling onto their mother's fur and drink her milk. After a few weeks, the young bats have fur too, and they start learning how to fly.

JUICE EXTRACTOR
Franquet's fruit bat sucks out the juices from rain forest fruits. It puts its lips around the fruit and bites into the flesh with its teeth. Then the bat squashes the fruit with its strong tongue and sucks out the juices.

The bat flexes these arm bones up and down to flap its wings.

GUESS WHAT?
This bat is also called the epauletted fruit bat. This is because the male has tufts of white fur on its shoulders, like the shoulder pieces (epaulettes) on a person's uniform.

SKINNY WING
Bats are the only mammals that can really fly. Their wings are made of an elastic membrane covered with skin. This is stretched between the four very long fingers on each hand. Bats lick their wings to keep them clean and in good condition for flying. On a hot day, they flap their wings like fans to keep themselves cool.

The skin is tightly stretched between the bones so that the wings are both light and strong.

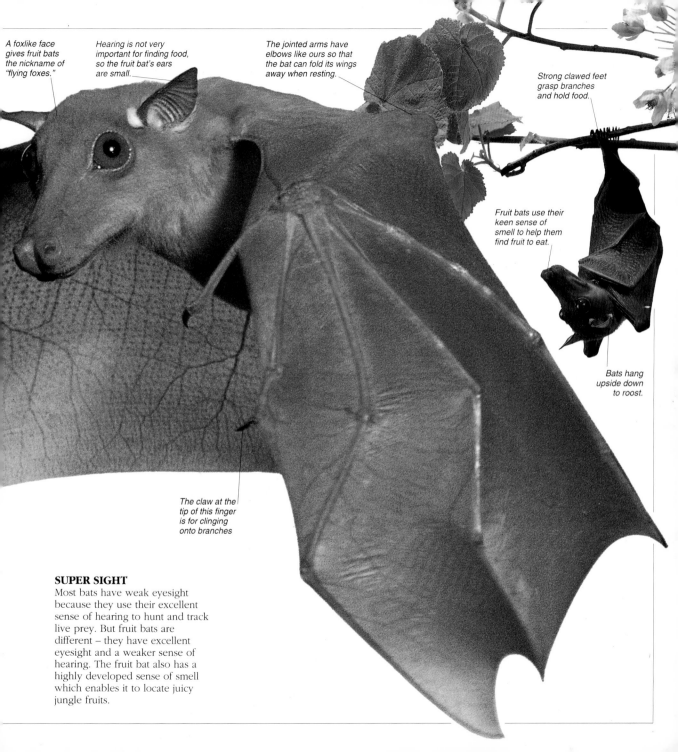

A foxlike face gives fruit bats the nickname of "flying foxes."

Hearing is not very important for finding food, so the fruit bat's ears are small.

The jointed arms have elbows like ours so that the bat can fold its wings away when resting.

Strong clawed feet grasp branches and hold food.

Fruit bats use their keen sense of smell to help them find fruit to eat.

Bats hang upside down to roost.

The claw at the tip of this finger is for clinging onto branches

SUPER SIGHT

Most bats have weak eyesight because they use their excellent sense of hearing to hunt and track live prey. But fruit bats are different – they have excellent eyesight and a weaker sense of hearing. The fruit bat also has a highly developed sense of smell which enables it to locate juicy jungle fruits.

HAIRY HUNTER

THIS LARGE, HAIRY SPIDER is not as dangerous as it looks. The curly-haired tarantula can kill small rodents, reptiles, or birds, but its bite is usually no more dangerous to people than a bee or wasp sting. During the day, tarantulas lurk under stones, bark, or leaves, or remain inside their silk-lined burrows on the forest floor. At night, they come out to hunt. Curly-haired tarantulas feel for prey in the darkness with two leglike pedipalps on the front of the body. Female tarantulas lay eggs, then cover them with a cocoon of silk for protection. The young spiderlings hatch inside the cocoon and emerge after they have molted once. As they grow into adults, they molt several more times. Female tarantulas like this one also molt when they are adults.

Spinnerets at the end of the abdomen produce silk.

Each hair is shaped like a tiny harpoon. The hooks along the sides cause itching and sneezing.

ITCHY HAIRS

The hairs on the tarantula's body can sense vibrations in the air. This helps the spider to find its way around and hunt in the dark. The hairs on its abdomen break off easily and irritate the skin of other animals, including humans. Tarantulas use their back legs to flick these hairs at enemies.

SPINNING SILK

At the end of the abdomen there are four spinnerets that the spider uses to spin silk. This silk is stronger than the same thickness of nylon rope or steel cable, and it is very stretchy.

GUESS WHAT?

The curly-haired tarantula is not a true tarantula, despite its name. It belongs to a family of bird-eating spiders. True tarantulas do not live in rain forests.

The body consists of two parts with a narrow waist, called a pedicel, in the middle.

Each leg is made up of seven parts, with two claws at the end and a tuft of hair underneath for extra grip.

POISON FANGS

Tarantulas are strong spiders. They pounce on their prey and hold it still with their pedipalps while their fangs inject poison. The poison paralyzes the prey and a special fluid from the spider's stomach digests the soft parts. The spider then sucks up the contents of its victim's body.

The eight simple eyes are tiny, so the spider has poor eyesight.

Pedipalps look like extra legs.

Huge fangs inject prey with poison.

DEADLY ORCHID

THIS EXTRAORDINARY insect is called an orchid mantis. It hides among the forest flowers, pretending to be an orchid, and waits for other, unsuspecting insects to land nearby. The mantis keeps quite still, and other creatures cannot see it because it is almost the same shape and color as the orchid. This keeps it safe from predators such as birds and lizards. Mantises feed mainly on grasshoppers, butterflies, moths, and flies, and they usually eat their prey alive. Sometimes mantises even eat each other, especially during mating, when the female often kills the male. A female mantis lays her eggs in a frothy mass. After three to six months, young larvae called nymphs hatch out of the eggs. They molt several times as they develop into adult mantises.

NIFTY NECK
This orchid mantis has such a flexible neck that it can turn its triangular-shaped head in almost any direction. This means that the mantis can spot enemies or prey without moving its body at all.

These antennae can feel and smell things.

Powerful jaws carve out chunks of the victim's flesh and chew them up until they are small enough to swallow.

Flaps on the legs make them look like flower petals.

Female mantises are about twice as large as the males.

PRAYING FOR A BITE
The mantis waits quietly on a flower until an insect lands. It rocks from side to side, swaying in the breeze like a flower. When at rest, it folds its legs in front of its face and looks as though it is praying. This is why mantises are also called praying mantises.

This female orchid mantis has pale-colored wings. The wings of a male are transparent.

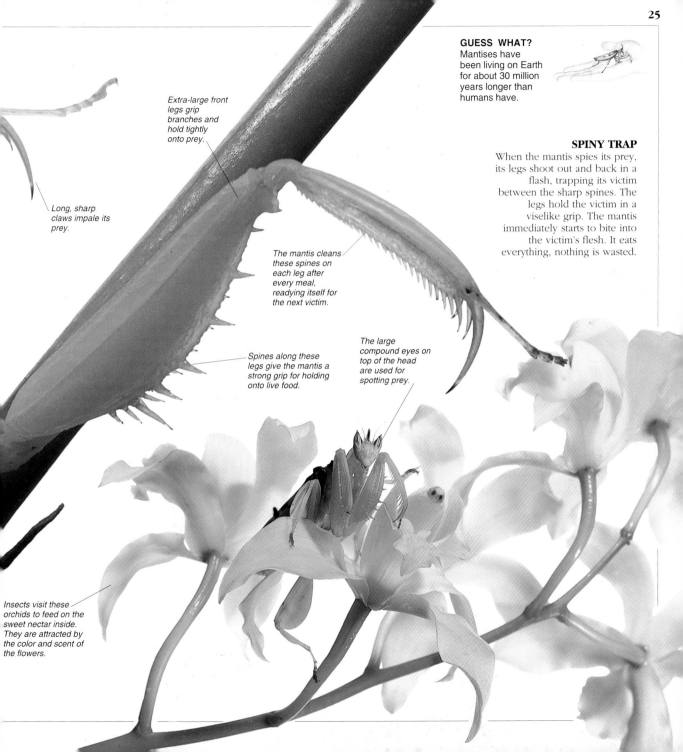

Long, sharp
claws impale its
prey.

Extra-large front
legs grip
branches and
hold tightly
onto prey.

The mantis cleans
these spines on
each leg after
every meal,
readying itself for
the next victim.

Spines along these
legs give the mantis a
strong grip for holding
onto live food.

The large
compound eyes on
top of the head
are used for
spotting prey.

Insects visit these
orchids to feed on the
sweet nectar inside.
They are attracted by
the color and scent of
the flowers.

GUESS WHAT?
Mantises have
been living on Earth
for about 30 million
years longer than
humans have.

SPINY TRAP
When the mantis spies its prey,
its legs shoot out and back in a
flash, trapping its victim
between the sharp spines. The
legs hold the victim in a
viselike grip. The mantis
immediately starts to bite into
the victim's flesh. It eats
everything, nothing is wasted.

RAINBOW BIRD

THIS CUVIER'S TOUCAN hops through branches high in the rain forest trees. It uses its long bill to reach berries and seeds on twigs that are too thin for it to perch on. By tossing back its head, it can flick food down its throat. Toucans are sociable birds and live in flocks, sometimes preening other toucans or offering them food. They also play games, such as throwing fruit to each other. Toucans do not build nests. Instead, they live in holes in tree trunks. Females lay as many as four white eggs and both parents share the task of keeping the eggs warm. When young toucans hatch, they are blind. Their feathers do not start to grow until they are nearly four weeks old. At about six weeks old, they have enough feathers to learn to fly and leave the nesting hole.

WAVING THE FLAG
The toucan uses its brightly colored bill like a flag to signal to other toucans. The colors help it to spot birds of its own kind and find a mate. Sometimes toucans use their bills to frighten off smaller birds so that they can steal other birds' eggs and young.

The large bill looks very heavy, but it is hollow and light.

Each toucan's bill is slightly different in color and pattern. This helps individual birds to recognize each other.

The passionfruit is one of the toucan's favorite foods. Its bright color makes it easy to find.

Serrated (notched) edges on the bill allow the toucan to bite off chunks of fruit.

When sleeping the toucan lays its huge bill along its back and covers it with its tail.

GUESS WHAT?
Newly hatched toucans have pads around each ankle, with spikes sticking out. The pads protect their feet from the rough wood and piles of discarded seeds inside the nesting hole.

LIGHT BITE
This huge bill is not as heavy as it looks. The outside is made of hard keratin, just like your fingernails, but the inside is hollow. Many crisscrossed bones help support the shape of the bill. Toucans use their bills to wrestle with each other, and the bill gets damaged sometimes.

Two of the toes point forward, and two point backward for extra grip on the branches of trees.

Toucans have sharp eyesight for spotting friends and foes.

The toucan's wide tail helps it balance while flying.

This white throat patch and the black body feathers look sort of like a penguin's "tuxedo."

FEATHER JACKET
The toucan's skin is very thin and sensitive. So, like other birds, it has feathers to keep it warm and dry. The feathers are strong, yet flexible and light for flying, and each one is a streamlined shape so that it does not slow the bird down.

Feathers cover the body.

THE HIGH LIFE

THESE RAIN FOREST ORCHIDS perch high on the branches of the tallest trees, where they are close to the sunlight. Plants that grow like this, on trees and other plants, are called epiphytes. These orchids have long, trailing roots that soak up moisture from the air. They also store food and water in swollen stems called pseudobulbs. Their colorful, scented flowers attract insects. The insects eat the nectar made by the flower and carry its pollen to other orchids. If an orchid flower receives pollen from another of the same kind, seeds may develop. Orchids produce thousands of tiny, light seeds that drift through the forest on the wind. If they land in a suitable spot, they grow into new plants.

Clusters of pollen are near the top of the flower.

POLLEN PARCELS

Most flowers have loose, dust-like pollen. But orchids have special clusters called pollinia consisting of thousands of pollen grains. Each cluster has a special pad at its base. The pad sticks to the head of a visiting insect, which carries it to another orchid flower.

Below the pollinia is the stigma (the tip of the female part).

The labellum of this flower forms a flat landing platform for insects.

Brightly colored petals to attract insects

FANTASTIC FLOWER

These orchids are unusual flowers. The stem of the male part (the stamen) and the stem of the female part (the style) are joined together in a central column. One of the orchid's petals, called the labellum, is a special shape, to attract the right kind of insect. The insect cannot get to the nectar it feeds on without becoming covered in pollen.

The flat, green leaves use sunlight to produce food for the plant.

There is a tough, waxy surface on each leaf to cut down water loss.

Each flower has three petals and three sepals. The sepals are longer and narrower than the petals.

STRONG SCENTS

In the rain forest, the light is dim. To help attract the insects which pollinate them, orchids often have a very strong scent. These orchids have sweet, heavy perfumes. Others smell of rotting meat, depending on the insects they need to attract.

GUESS WHAT?

There are more than 25,000 kinds of orchids in the world. Three quarters of these live by perching on other plants. A single orchid plant may produce up to a million seeds.

INDEX

GLOSSARY

Abdomen *the rear part of the body*
Antennae *a pair of feelers*
Cocoon *a bag which an insect pupa spins from silk for protection*
Exoskeleton *a tough covering on the body, made of a substance called chitin*
Fang *a large, pointed tooth*
Labellum *the liplike part of certain flowers and insects*
Larva *the young, grublike stage of an animal such as an insect*
Mammal *a warm-blooded animal such as a mouse or rabbit*
Metamorphosis *the transformation from a larva to an adult*
Molt *to shed the skin or exoskeleton*

Mucus *a slimy, often poisonous substance which certain animals produce*
Pedipalps *the leglike parts on the head of a spider or scorpion*
Proboscis *the long, strawlike mouthpart of an animal such as a butterfly*
Pupa/chrysalis *the resting stage between a larva and an adult insect*
Roost *to rest or sleep, often in a high place*
Sepal *one of the outer parts of a flower that protect the bud*
Thorax *the middle part of the body, containing the heart and lungs*
Trachea *a windpipe, for breathing*
Vibrations *tiny movements in air, in water, or underground*